IF ANY MAN MINISTER

IF ANY MAN MINISTER

The 1950 Warrack Lectures on Preaching

E. D. Jarvis, D.D.

If any man minister let him do it as of the ability which God giveth.

I PET IV. 11.

LONDON
HODDER AND STOUGHTON

FIRST PRINTED 1951

*Made and printed in Great Britain for
Hodder and Stoughton Limited, by
The Camelot Press Limited,
London and Southampton*

To
MY WIFE

CONTENTS

INTRODUCTION

I REGARD it as a great honour to have been invited to give the Warrack Lectures on Preaching.

I was encouraged to accept the invitation by being assured that I should address myself specifically to students, and should speak to them out of my own experience.

Accordingly, these are the limits that I have set myself in what I am going to say. It is open to anyone to think that I am too elementary and too personal. I deliberately take that risk.

I begin by expressing my indebtedness to my three congregations in Penicuik, London and Glasgow. What I know about preaching and the work of the ministry I have learned by practising on them. They have always thought better of me than I have deserved. They have been extraordinarily patient with my faults. Because of their loyalty to the Church and their interest in the things of the Spirit, they have set a standard which has been to me always an inspiration, and quite frequently a rebuke.

The lessons I have learned from them, and am still learning, fall naturally under these headings:

1. The Preacher as Evangelist.
2. The Preacher as Craftsman.

3. The Preacher as Teacher.
4. The Preacher as Minister.
5. The Preacher as Man.

I shall deal with these subjects in that order.

––––––

Such was my spoken introduction to the lectures, when I delivered them. Now that they are being printed, I should like to express my thanks to the Principals, Professors, and Students of New College, Edinburgh, and of St. Mary's College, St. Andrews, in whose hearing they were spoken. It greatly increased the pleasure I had in being Warrack Lecturer that, in the case of both Colleges I was revisiting the scenes, and reviving the memories of my own student years. I should also like to record my indebtedness to Miss Freda Anderson, who typed the lectures, first for my own use when I spoke them, and subsequently for the printers.

I

THE PREACHER AS EVANGELIST

I

THE PREACHER AS EVANGELIST

IN addressing myself to the consideration of the preacher as evangelist, let me say that I am not thinking of the preacher of special gifts who undertakes special missions. I have no such equipment and have had no such experience. I am thinking of the minister who is faced, week by week, by the same people (or would be, if they all came to church regularly, which unfortunately they do not).

Who are they, and what can we do for them? Surely they have heard the Gospel often enough? The answer is not only that there is in the Gospel incomparable and inexhaustible nourishment for all our souls, and we can never have enough of it: but also that we need constant encouragement both to believe it and to live by it.

Look at your congregation. They are men and women surrounded by a great mystery. They are living in a world too complicated for them to understand, and they need a key to unlock its meaning. They have one brief life to live under the sun. It should be a good and a full life, but it is so very easy to make it otherwise. They have their hopes and aspirations, but life itself seems so often to put obstacles in the way of their fulfilment. They appear to be self-sufficient and even, it may be, self-complacent, but, under the surface, they are at least vaguely uneasy, missing they know not what. Objectively considered and compared with the less responsible members of society, they are not great sinners, and certainly no greater sinners than we who preach to them. But they have regrets and fears which they cannot get the better of, and they have thoughts and desires which they find it difficult to control. They are living in times when the foundations of the world they have grown up in are being sapped, and they need some sure standing ground for their feet. They see age-old sanctions and standards being jettisoned, and they need a star to guide them. Is it not true of them that they are, more often than would appear, acutely conscious of their own solitariness, and that they crave for understanding, fellowship, and love?

That description is far from exhaustive, but it will serve to show that there is a wide range of need to be met. How indeed can it ever be met? Not certainly by anything that we by ourselves can say or do. All that we can hope for is to prepare the way for God to come in, and to deal with it Himself.

I do not need, I am sure, to persuade you that that is so. It is the Gospel which has answered *our* questions, has kept alive *our* aspirations, has combated *our* sense of futility and unworthiness, has supplied *our* need for courage and faith and love and peace. It is, therefore, the Gospel which we must preach with all the persuasiveness and power at our command.

It might appear, as I have suggested, that, in preaching the Gospel for many years to the same people, we might, sooner or later, dull their interest and become bored ourselves.

Certainly, if we had to rely on our own mental and spiritual resources, that would be the inevitable result. But the Old and New Testaments, where we find the Gospel set forth, are so full and so rich that we never exhaust them. As the years pass, we see deeper into their meaning, scholarship supplies new interpretations, experience and reading provide fresh illustrations, and week by week the barrel of meal is replenished and the cruse of oil has not failed. As our own minds are stimulated and our own souls are refreshed, we have something to pass on that God can and does use.

I do not base that statement on any measure of thanks expressed by members of our congregations. Sometimes they do tell us that they have been helped, and that is, of course, encouraging. But I base it rather on this, that sometimes, as we preach, there comes a profound hush over our hearers, and we have the sense of something imminent, and of something actually happening. It is then we know that God is getting, and taking, His chance to establish and to confirm a saving relationship with men and women. That is the objective we should always have in mind as we prepare and as we preach our sermons. Our business is just this—to prepare the way of the Lord.

What texts and passages in the Old and New Testaments are the most likely to give us the chance to do this, and how best may we deal with them?

There are those texts and passages which are the very core of the Gospel, which bring us face to face with Christ, and especially with His Cross. Nothing ever produces the hush I have mentioned like preaching Christ and Him crucified. And no way of preaching Christ and Him crucified can ever be so effective as that which comes warm and living out of our own experience. We must search our own souls, think our own thoughts, and employ to the full our own imaginations.

We should be encouraged to do this by remembering that a lot of water has flowed under the bridges since the Apostle Paul sought to plumb the depth of meaning in the Cross by using analogies drawn from the Jewish sacrificial system, the contemporary slave-markets and the Roman law courts. Very naturally, Paul thought in legal terms, such as judgment, condemnation, advocacy, justification, remission. It is possible that these are the only categories, even now, that are adequate to illustrate and explain these, the greatest of mysteries—the reconciliation of the human soul with its Maker, and the gift of a new spirit through Christ. I do not know. But I know that the Cross can exercise its unique power without our being able to explain how it does it. Somehow, it is not any explanation of it, but the sheer impact of the Cross itself that moves, and shrives, and changes the soul of the beholder. Here is the sin of man and here is the love of God: here is the place where we realise that in a just and morally governed universe we have nothing to say for ourselves: here is the One who, by His self-sacrifice, pleads with us to re-order our lives and to give them over to the purposes of God; here is the place of decision as to who shall be our master; here is the hammer with which God would break our hard hearts; here is at once God's defeat and the assurance of His final victory; here is the love of God come to haunt the world until men surrender to it and live. It is not the time-worn phrases that will bring home the meaning of the Cross to our people: at least, if they *are* used, they must be given something of the freshness they had when they were first minted.

Modern translations help us to bring our own thoughts and imaginations into play, and we should use them constantly. Let me give an instance of how even the alteration of a single word may set the wheels in motion. In Rom. viii. 1, the Authorised Version reads: "There is, therefore, now no *condemnation* to them which are in Christ Jesus." Dr. Moffatt's translation runs: "Thus there is no *doom* now." It was, I confess, that simple change of one word that lit up the Apostle's meaning for me. There is much talk of men being doomed by this or that fact or circumstance, by heredity, environment, weakness of character and will. They are no longer "doomed" by anything whatever, once the saving and enabling grace of Christ enters their souls. The modern translations—particularly, to my mind, Phillips' *Letters to Young Churches*—have much help to give in kindling our imaginations and giving wings to our thoughts.

Commentaries are, of course, necessary tools which should be in constant use. They not only suggest interpretations, but keep these on sound lines. Yet we must never be afraid to go beyond any commentary we may have consulted. I remember sitting down before "And the veil of the Temple was rent in twain"—an event recorded, you remember, as having accompanied the Crucifixion. The commentaries interpreted that symbol of the rent veil to mean that, henceforward, not the High Priest only could, once a year, enter into the Holy of Holies, but that all men could, at any time, have free access to the presence of God. That is certainly a valuable assurance. But then it struck me: if, now that the veil has been rent, we can go in, cannot God also come out? I felt at once that there was something living in that idea for my mind to work on. I called the sermon "God makes His Escape," and I pictured this result of the Crucifixion, that God had emerged from the mystery that had surrounded Him, from the realm of magic and taboo, from the control of priests and the confines of temples made with hands. He was free, henceforward, to meet us in every circumstance of our lives and in every condition of our souls. I felt, as I developed the thought, that I had been led to a fresh angle from which to preach an eternal truth. I commend to you the advantage of thinking your own thoughts and using your own imaginative insight in dealing with even the greatest themes.

These great themes, and the great texts which enshrine them, are, of course, already familiar to most of your hearers, and you may feel diffident about going over such familiar ground. Yet there is value even in announcing a great familiar text, just because your hearers will wonder what you are going to say about it, and they will give you their undivided attention at least for a minute or two till they find out. You must "cash in," as we say, on this initial interest.

Your text is, say, John iii. 16, "For God so loved the world that He gave His only begotten Son, that whosoever believeth in Him should not perish, but have everlasting life." Many thousands of sermons have been preached on this text. What have *you* to say about it? Nothing that has not been said a thousand times before, but the new factor in the situation is *you*. What does the text say to *you*?

I looked up a sermon I preached on the text, to find what it had said to me. And this is what I found. I do not say there is anything wonderful in the ideas, but the point is they were my own. The text gave me, I find:

1. *A God to believe in*

A God with a big heart. We know something of what love means; we do love one or two. But how many we barely tolerate, and how many prejudices—class, national, racial—we have to fight in our little human hearts! God loves the world. Narrow minds and little hearts are not for those who believe in God the Father of Jesus Christ.

2. *A world to live in*

Not a world where we have the right to exploit our gifts and station for selfish ends; not a world where any man (or any nation) has the right to wade through rivers of blood to achieve power and wealth: but a world for which Christ died. If we live in the same world as Christ lived in, we know what is required of us in service and sacrifice.

3. *A life to share in*

A life full of interest and adventure; a life with meaning and value in it; a life centred, not in self, but in God, not in the things of time, but in the things of eternity. Our lives, here and now, may have an eternal quality in them so that death has no power over them. Is not quality of life more than anything else the surest promise of immortality?

Under such heads—a God to believe in, a world to live in, a life to share in—how much that is right and important about the content and application of the Christian faith can be said.

Apart from the great texts, there is no better way of seeing Christ than through the eyes of those who saw Him in the days of His flesh, and there is no surer way than that of coming face to face both with ourselves and Him. What did the good centurion see in Him that gave him the greater faith than any found in Israel? What did the woman who anointed His feet with ointment see that made her dissolve in tears? And what did Zaccheus see that he became a reformed character and salvation had come to his house?

These are questions for the answers to which you need not consult commentaries, Or, if you do, you need not be tied to what they say.

Take the case of the centurion at the Cross who said: "Truly this man was the Son of God. . . ." I dare say one might spend time on the theological implications of the phrase "the Son of God," and, incidentally, read into it meanings which could not possibly have occurred to the centurion. The centurion was no theologian. He was a soldier, skilled and accustomed to size up men in barracks and on the battlefield. He knew himself well enough to know he would not, in like circumstances, have shown such courage and endurance.

His spirit rose up to salute a master spirit. Do we need to ask more of any man than that he should look at Christ on the Cross and look longer than he is accustomed to look? The one qualification the centurion had was that he looked at Christ for a whole day, and no man who looks at Christ long enough can fail to see One who is of a commanding stature, or forbear, as I believe, to confess: "Truly this Man was the Son of God."

If we can let our people see those men and women of whom we are told so little, but can know so much, if we can let our people see what they saw, then they will make their own confession as Peter did at Caesarea, and pay their own tribute as the centurion did at the Cross. Only as these Biblical characters live again for us will they become alive to our congregations, and only as we ourselves see Christ through their eyes will others likewise, hearing us, see Him.

There is no good preaching that does not deal in pictures. Do not be afraid of pictures. Jesus was not afraid of them. His parables are pictures. You will find, as I have found, that there is an interest that can be felt as you hold up a simple picture which illustrates the Gospel. The Psalms in particular rival the Gospels themselves in the number of pictures they provide. Take one verse of Ps. xxiii and see what it conjures up before your imagination. Let the verse be: "He restoreth my soul." Ask yourself, "How is the soul restored?" The answer is:

1. By a change of air and scene.

The Good Physician prescribes that. The soul's native air is often denied it. That native air is not the polluted air of the world, but the clean, bracing air of the heavenly country. If we go apart and rest awhile with Christ, as He invites us to do, our souls are restored.

2. By being cleansed, in something of the way pictures are restored when the grime of years is removed from them. How colour and definition come back to character and life at the touch of Christ, who alone can forgive us our sins and cleanse us from all unrighteousness! It takes a while to do, but it is done, and only He can do it.

3. By having qualities that rightly belong to the soul given back to us, even as lost property is restored to its rightful owner. Faith, hope, courage, self-respect, and self-control are ours again through Christ. He is the great finder and restorer of that which is lost to us and to God.

Such thoughts may sound very simple. Do not be afraid of being simple: only be afraid of being superficial. Congregations do not thank us for being either dull or difficult. What is simple to listen to is often very difficult to produce, and what is difficult for our congregations to follow is frequently so because we have not spent enough time and effort on our preparation. My congregations have confirmed an impression which was early made upon me in my ministry: that they like a simple sermon best, and get the most benefit from it. They probably do not know, as I do, that these simple sermons are often the hardest to come by.

Speaking of pictures, there is virtue in taking two companion or contrasting texts, when we find them, and giving two companion or contrasting pictures.

Take, for example, "There was no room for them in the Inn" and set over against that: "In My Father's house are many mansions." There you have portrayed, on the one hand, man's inhospitality to God, the refusal to give Him any place, however small, in our intimate lives, and, on the other, the great hospitality of God experienced daily, and expressed here by Jesus, who speaks of the home prepared for us when our life on earth is done.

Or, take Pilate washing his hands in a basin, and contrast that with the other picture of Jesus taking a towel and a basin, and washing His disciples' feet. Do not these two basins symbolise two attitudes? How usual an attitude to wash the hands of responsibility, saying, "It is no business of mine," "I couldn't care less," and how many blots and stains can only be cleansed by lowly and self-forgetting service, with love and pity in our hearts! You have been holding up two pictures which are at once recognised as lifelike, and they will not readily be forgotten.

You can see that I give the widest meaning to the name "Evangelist," and that there is no special kind of text that we must choose in order to preach the Gospel. We may indeed take texts that have no spiritual significance in themselves, and find that they illustrate the Gospel in a most effective way.

Take, for example, Acts xxvii. 29: "Then fearing lest we should have fallen upon rocks, they cast four anchors out of the stern, and wished for the day." We need not go to the sea in ships to know occasions when we are in danger, and circumstances are rather desperate for our souls. Have we four anchors? We have—

1. God knows.
2. God cares.
3. God has promised.
4. God is able.

Let these anchors go, and we can ride out any storm. Such is the testimony of Christians who have done it for twenty centuries.

I do not hold with spiritualising Scripture which, on the face of it, has no spiritual reference: the analogy must be very obvious. I think it is obvious here.

You can see also, I hope, that the greatest importance attaches to the evangelist himself. I shall be speaking later on the preacher as a man. Meanwhile, I shall content myself with these remarks:

First, obvious sincerity in the preacher is of more importance than carefully rounded sentences. Sentences look after themselves if you know what you want to say, if you are describing something you see, and if the fire is burning within you. Before your subject can possess others, it must first possess you.

Second, what you put of yourself into your sermon is of more importance than what you put in of other people. Few of us are likely to be original thinkers and we must use other men's brains, but there is nothing so ineffective as too-frequent quotations or as handing out material that has not been passed through our own minds till it has become our own.

Third, an object for our preaching is as necessary as a subject for it. Whatever be our text, our aim should always be, before we are done, to leave our hearers face to face with God. That this should be possible is the only excuse for, and the greatest encouragement in, preaching. The simplest witness may do what the most eloquent discourse fails to do.

And last: It is better to say "we" than "you," "come" than "go." It is better to confess than to criticise, better to encourage than to scold. Identify yourself with the people you are preaching to, as a fellow sinner and a fellow struggler with them. It is absolutely imperative for a preacher to put himself alongside his hearers, and not to talk to them, as it were, from a height. There should be no doubt but that he is seeking humbly to share with them what, by the grace of God, he himself has found, and that he has no other feeling about the most outrageous sinner than "There go I, but for the grace of God."

II

THE PREACHER AS CRAFTSMAN

II

THE PREACHER AS CRAFTSMAN

WE are to deal with the preparation and delivery of the sermon. Though I shall have more to say about the preparation than about the delivery, that is not the measure of the relative importance of these two aspects of the craft of preaching. After we have produced a sermon on paper, either in full or in notes, it has to be conveyed by the living voice to the people who are there to listen to it. The importance of this second step is obvious.

When we set about preparing a sermon, we have to fix on a subject. Sometimes it is very difficult to decide on one, and an inordinate amount of time may be spent in making up one's mind. In the next lecture I shall be speaking of the advantages of giving addresses in a series. One of the advantages is that the question of what we are to preach about need not worry us every week. Apart from that, the Christian year, on many an occasion, comes to our help, and we should make the fullest use of it. Following a scheme of Scripture readings throughout the year is a practice to be commended, since the lessons for the next Sunday may suggest a text or subject. Special occasions come at intervals, as, for example, Remembrance

Sunday, or there may be a call to preach to specific needs which have emerged in the lives of members of our congregation. All such considerations narrow the field of search. In the light of them we know, at least, what we are looking for, and that makes things a little easier. As, however, there are times when none of these sources of supply prove helpful, I must offer some suggestions as to how we may avoid the nervous strain of living from hand to mouth in the matter of sermon-production.

A friend who was no mean exponent of the craft told me once that he found the getting of sermons as good fun as fishing. I would not know—for I do not fish. Over everything he read or saw, whether in the Bible or out of it, he cast, as it were, a fly. There was often a tug—that was an idea, an illustration. Out it came and in it went to his notebook as into a fishing basket. He had found a heading for a new sermon, or something to add under a heading already there. When he wanted a subject for Sunday, he turned up his notebook, and sometimes, not only the subject, but the line of treatment and illustrations as well, were there, ready to be worked up.

The late Dr. R. F. Horton tells us in one of his books that he too followed this practice, and he adds this, which is illuminating: "Subjects were always there, pressing to be dealt with: the only embarrassment was to know which to select for each occasion. But, as time went on, I observed that the selection also came to me. Circumstances, or the experience of life, or some particular demand, showed clearly that *this* subject must be taken for Sunday morning, and *that* for the evening. Sometimes I could have answered the question why I took that subject, sometimes I could not. But, again and again, I found that there were people in the congregation who were startled by the fact that the subject was just what they needed. They had come to church with a question in their minds, and the answer was direct and unmistakable."

I am sure most preachers have had such experiences. We do not sit down by ourselves to write our sermons, and the more conscious we are of that, and the more we depend on the guidance of the Holy Spirit, the more frequent such experiences are.

But my point now is that in the end notebooks and cuttings and keeping track of your reading in some systematic way save a great deal of time and trouble.

In the event of no suggestions coming from this source, I commend to you a practice of the late Professor H. R. Mackintosh, who used to say to us, his students, that he found *Daily Light* a help, not only in suggesting texts, but in gathering together what the Bible, as a whole, has to say on any particular theme. There are other devotional books of a similar kind which are, no doubt, equally valuable.

The selection of a subject may be dramatised as I once heard Dr. Alexander Whyte, that prince of preachers, do it in the little church at Logiepert near Montrose. Forty years ago we had walked on a bright summer Sunday morning from Montrose to hear him. He began his sermon by telling us he had been lying in bed in the Manse, wondering what he should tell the people of Logiepert. One after another the great figures of the Bible came to his bedside and said, "Tell the people of Logiepert this, that and the other." Moses came; Elijah came; Paul came. So many I remember. Then followed Luther, Calvin, William Law—all with their characteristic messages which they asked him to tell the people of Logiepert. Last came a little man with a gentle face and a quiet voice. His name? Hosea. He said: "Tell the people of Logiepert about the Love of God." And that is what Dr. Whyte proceeded to do. Perhaps the real lesson from that story is the best way to find subjects for sermons is to have a well stored mind, and a vivid imagination! Another lesson is that it is not so much that you have to find a subject, as that a subject has to find you.

When that has happened—and, say, a text has detached itself from the Old or New Testament and you are to prepare a sermon on it—what are you to do with it? It will not be enough to discover its original meaning and to relate it to its context. *The* important thing is to ask: What relevance has it for to-day? What is its preaching value? You must answer such questions before you do anything else. You are not going to write an essay or a theological treatise: you are going to address people who have neither your special interests nor your special training. You must talk about things that are real to them, things that affect them in their daily lives, things that are relevant to the world they know, and to the times they are living in.

For example, you have taken, let us say, the story of the man in the country of the Gergesenes who was possessed by devils (Matt. viii). Are you going to give a dissertation on devil possession? Are you going to explain those pigs rushing to destruction in the sea? No doubt there is material here for learned disquisitions on devil-possession and the miracles of Jesus. I do not think the majority of your congregation would really be much the wiser for these, or that they are proper subjects for a single sermon. But you observe that the last words of the story are: "And they besought Him that He would depart out of their coasts." What an extraordinary thing, you think. One would have supposed that—

1. For the sake of the poor devil-possessed men and women, of whom there were great numbers (i.e. *for humanity's sake*), they would have asked Him to stay. And—

2. For their own sakes also (i.e. *out of self-interest*)—since apparently the devil-possessed made the roads unsafe—they would have asked Him to stay.

Surely people to-day would not, in similar circumstances, ask Him to go away? No? Is the sentiment of humanity so strong, then, or self-interest so wise and wide-awake? Is it not the case that men think they can get on very well without Christ although they are living in a world where nations, let alone individuals, are possessed with devils, and where it is increasingly dangerous, and indeed impossible, for men to move about the world freely and safely on their lawful occasions?

When you have seen the relevance of this story to present-day conditions, then you have made a real beginning to your sermon preparation. You have found something that will preach.

What happens after you have found that something will depend on yourself, and on the way your mind works. You may be one who can decide at once your line of treatment, or you may be one who has to make several abortive attempts before the right line comes to you. But, whatever your type or skill, if the mechanical, mass-production effect which characterises, I fear, many sermons is to be avoided, a sermon must grow in obedience to the nature of the text itself. There must not be a stereotyped pattern to which our treatment must conform. We must sit down before our text, let it speak to us, and let it yield up its own message. That is the only way in which vitality and variety can be imparted to our preaching.

Let me give some examples of varied treatment of texts. Your text settled, you may find it is almost a ready-made sermon as it stands. Say it is Gen. xxvi. 25: "And he builded an altar there, and called upon the name of the Lord, and pitched his tent there: and there Isaac's servants digged a well." Tent, well, and altar. People demand the first two, but what about the third? Where does religion come in the lives of the majority of people?

Or it is a phrase in the text that stands out and has something to say to you. For example, John i. 12. "To them gave He power to become the sons of God." "Power to become" is the phrase, and you think of how discipline, *esprit de corps*, leadership in Navy, Army and Air Force have made giants of ordinary men and of how there is power in Christ, by discipline, *esprit de corps*, and leadership to do the same for us.

Or it is a single word that lays hold on your mind, like the word "satisfied" in Ps. lxv. 4: We shall be satisfied with the goodness of Thy house." "Satisfied" you think—*satis*, 'enough'—enough of what? And there you are with—

1. A purpose that is high enough.
2. A happiness that is deep enough.
3. A love that is strong and enduring enough.

Are there not those in your congregation who are missing the purpose, happiness and love that can satisfy? Are there not vast multitudes looking in the wrong places for the purpose, happiness and love they need? Are not these the gifts God's house offers to us all?

Or the text can be put, as it stands, to different uses. . . . Take Matt. xvi. 26: "For what is a man profited, if he shall gain the whole world, and lose his own soul?" That solemn and searching question can become—

1. An epitaph, that describes the end of the man of ambition.
2. A danger signal which we ignore at our peril.
3. A staff to lean on when the going is hard, and we are greatly tempted.

I do not suggest that these illustrations make the best use of the texts I have dealt with so summarily. But I do suggest that, if we let the text sink in and do its own germinating in our minds, a natural and suitable line of treatment will follow, and we shall escape the ever-present peril of dealing in a mechanical way with words expressive of living truth.

What emerges when we have so let our text sink in? Heads; perhaps different aspects of one idea: perhaps different situations or people to whom the text applies —perhaps steps in an argument. Two or three heads, or sometimes, not often, four, with something inevitable and inescapable about them. These are certainly the best kind, because they are the kind that stick.

Some preachers seem to despise heads. They may put them down for their own guidance, but they do not pass them on to their hearers. Whether this is a good thing or not depends, I dare say, on the kind of sermon. But on the whole I think it advisable to mention in preaching what our heads are. How many people come away from church with the vaguest ideas of how a sermon has been developed. Isn't there a story about President Calvin Coolidge to the effect that his wife asked him what the preacher had been preaching on, and he replied, "Sin." "And what did he say about it?" "He was against it." . . . I expect the preacher in that instance did not say what his heads were!

Needless to say, I do not mean the kind of heads that apocryphal stories ascribe to Negro preachers. Nor do I mean the alliterative kind, "the last, the least and the lost" kind, though sometimes there is a place for them. I mean heads as satisfying and as inevitable as these, which were passed on to me years ago by a friend, the text being from the Epistle of James iv. 14: "For what is your life?" Though I have turned to that question often and have preached on it more than once, I have never been able to get past the heads I was then given. All James says is that "it is even a vapour that appeareth for a little time and then vanisheth away." Very true, but not the full answer of the Bible on the question. That full answer is—at least, I think it is:

1. It is a gift.
2. It is an opportunity.
3. It is a beginning.

Simple heads indeed, but can you improve on them? Will you be able to forget them?

Take another text about life. (Life is an inexhaustible topic. Speak on it and people will listen. Is it not the only topic? Christ's promises are life—abundant life, eternal life.) The text is Gal. ii. 20: "The life which I now live in the flesh I live by the faith of the Son of God who loved me and gave Himself for me."

What kind of life did the Apostle live in the flesh by the faith of the Son of God? Think of his sufferings, his missionary strategy, his final sacrifice. . . . Sit back in your chair and see the life of the Apostle roll out as a panorama before you. You cannot but conclude that his life was one in which—

1. Nothing was too high to be attempted.
2. Nothing was too hard to be endured.
3. Nothing was too good to be hoped for. And
4. Nothing was too precious to be given away.

If that is not a fairly full and accurate description of the kind of life Paul lived by the faith of the Son of God, and the kind of life we are all called to live by the same faith, I am greatly mistaken. These are heads that stick: at least they stick to me. It is heads that stick we want and we should take pains to get them.

Having got our heads, and some notes written down under each, we make a start to write the sermon out. There may be, first, a few words of introduction, or we may plunge straight in. Never a page or two of background: never ancient history for an opening. Unless we make contact with our hearers in the beginning, we may never make contact with them at all. They are not likely to be interested in the Israelites, wandering or otherwise, or in the voyages of St. Paul, or in the Sanhedrin—however much you may be.

For example, we are dealing with the interview between Jesus and Nicodemus, and our text is John iii. 10: "Jesus answered and said unto him: Art thou a Master of Israel, and knowest not these things?" Why not begin: "This is a question which we might quite well ask of many who are masters to-day, masters of arts, doctors of science, technical experts, leaders in business and in affairs of state. This is a day of many masters in many Israels." Jesus asked such a master long ago if he did not know that a new birth, a new spirit, is the primary necessity. Do these contemporary masters know it, and know where the new spirit comes from?

There is the beginning, and there is the subject of your sermon.

That illustrates not only, I think, how immediate contact can be made with one's audience, but it also illustrates this: that we ought to be able to give a succinct outline of a sermon before ever we start to write. Certainly we ought to be able to give such an outline once the sermon is written. The same friend who told me that he found getting sermons was like fishing told me also that he went, by invitation, to a certain theological college in order to help the students to prepare for a mission in a great city. In preparation for his coming, the men were asked to have an address written, which he could go over with them. At the first meeting of his class, he looked down the list of their names, selected one of them, and asked him to tell the rest what it was he meant to say to the people when he spoke to them from the pulpit. The student proceeded to read his prepared address. My friend interrupted him. "Don't read," he said. "Just tell us what it is you are going to say." "Oh! I couldn't do that," said the man, "I have it written here." "Well but, you see," said the instructor, "it is going to take a long time to get through the whole class this way. Tell us, do, the gist of what you have written." It was no use: the student either could not or would not, and so the MS. was read. As might be expected, it was a theological essay, technically worded, difficult to follow, reminiscent of the lectures and the language of his professors, and in particular of the Principal, whose name was a household word in theological circles at that time, and still is. Of course, that kind of address was useless for the purpose in view.

So, right from the start, we should aim at producing sermons which will be so simple in their construction, so logical in their arrangement, so relevant in all their parts to getting our message home to our hearers that we shall always be able to carry at least the outline in our heads, go over the outline before we step into the pulpit, and give anyone who cares to ask beforehand, a fair idea of what we are going to say. If we cannot do that, then is it likely that any of our hearers will be able to say what we did say, when we have done?

Illustrations are, of course, a great help to our memories as well as necessary ingredients in our sermons. A distinguished Methodist gave me a good idea of his own practice in sermon-building. He said he built his sermons as a mason builds a wall, as sound and solid as he knew how. Then he looked at it critically. A wall is not a very interesting object. A house is, and what makes the difference between a wall and a house, as you look at it, is windows. Windows give life to what would be a dead and dull wall. So he proceeded to put windows into his sermon and to add some little decoration of phrase or allusion. We need illustrations: not too many; not too literary; not poetry unless in small doses, the meaning clear and the point plain. A poet as difficult as Browning has to be handled with care. We need illustrations, the homelier and the more familiar the better; the more scriptural the better, some would say; illustrations out of our own experience, from our own observation and reading. We need illustrations, but never with a view to showing how widely we have read, and always, if possible, illustrations which are our own and are not lifted out of books of illustrations. An illustration which really brings what we are saying to life is a precious possession: a pleasure to find and a pleasure to use. The sooner we get into the habit of bringing all our reading and all our observation of men and things under tribute to our preaching, the better. It is no easy task to have to produce two, three or even more addresses per week for years on end, and all the time to keep our congregation interested listeners. To be able to illustrate what we have to say, and to keep finding new illustrations of the old truths we have to preach, is one of the best ways of surviving what is, quite obviously, a gruelling test.

I need not remind you that our congregations are not so fond of long sermons as they used to be, and there is truth in what the bishop said to the curate who asked him what he should preach about. "About God and twenty minutes," he said. It is not, of course, a hard and fast rule that we preach for twenty minutes, but it is wise not to break it too often. The end should come, not because your time is up, but because you have made your point. Should not the closing sentences be carefully prepared to sum up what we have been saying, to bring some invitation, some challenge as from God Himself? The sermon has ended, as it ought to end, if it is the most natural thing in the world to turn to prayer—not to a collect hurriedly spoken, and better than to "Now to God the Father, God the Son, and God the Holy Spirit"—to a very few sentences, which rise to the lips almost unbidden and quite extemporaneously, in which you express the effect the sermon has had upon yourself. That is the best indication of the kind of effect it will have had on your hearers.

So far I have been assuming that the way to prepare a sermon is to write it out in full. In the earlier years of one's ministry, I have no doubt that that is the best practice. Later on, in a large church with a multiplicity of demands on one's time, it may not be possible. Yet the earlier habit will not have been wasted. Personally, I find it quite impossible, except on occasion, to write out a sermon in full. The best use to which I can put the time available is to get my line clear, so that I can move from point to point, get illustrations, prepare the opening and the ending, and write fairly full notes. I find it much easier to clothe my thoughts in words when keyed up for preaching than I do when sitting at my desk. I do not commend this as the best method for everyone to adopt, but I do say that whether we have a full manuscript before us in the pulpit, or notes, the more we look at our congregation and the less we look at the book-board the better. For, if we look at the people they will look at us. I also say that we should always leave room for extempore speech, for asides, for alterations of phrase and emphasis. If there is living contact between preacher and congregation, thought as well as utterance is bound to be stimulated. So why keep rigidly to what you have prepared?

May I also add that the more of the platform manner we adopt in preaching, the better. We must get rid of the kind of blanketing effect so often produced by putting on a Geneva gown. I have known men who could be most interesting in conversation and on the platform, who, in the pulpit and preaching a sermon were extremely dull. There is no real reason why that should be so, if we remember that religion is the most exciting thing in the world. Preaching that even remotely suggests that it is a sad or boring or pedestrian thing is giving a quite false impression. We have a lot to learn from other public speakers, from journalists and others who address either written or spoken words to a popular audience.

If you agree with me about that, then you will agree with me also, that voice and manner in preaching are of immense importance. I dare say we cannot help the quality of our voices, but we can at least make the best of what we have. We can learn to produce them so as not to affect adversely either our own throats or our hearers' ears. There is every reason why, even if we cannot hope to get their results, we should pay as much attention to voice-production as actors do. We can learn to breathe properly, to use our lips, and to open our throats. Hearing some men speak and sing, one is inclined to say, "That man should have his throat cut." We can take trouble over pronunciation and give full value to our final d's and t's, without becoming pedantic about it and adding a short 'a' to them, as I have heard men do more than once. We can practise getting light and shade into our speech; we can learn neither to shout nor to be inaudible, and we do well to guard against that bugbear, the "pulpit" voice. Easy, natural speech, pleasant to listen to, with as few eccentricities as possible is what we must aim at. A local accent may be a charming and attractive possession: it may also be a serious handicap. There is no need to be ashamed of being Scots any more than of being English, but there is every reason why we should be ashamed of making the English language sound ugly. We have a lovely message to utter, and the way we utter it should be as worthy of it as study and training can make it.

I am not going to say much more about this aspect of preaching. One can so readily detect faults in the speech of others, while remaining blind to defects in one's own. Like the teacher who was trying to eradicate glottal stops. "Don't say bu'er; say butter," said the teacher. The pupil did so. "That's be'er," said the teacher. It is a good thing to have a critic at home to point out one's faults, and it is a pity that young preachers cannot be provided with not too adoring wives and with sufficiently grown-up families, who would help them, by frank criticism, from the very beginning. Then perhaps we should have "God" and "Psalms" pronounced as they ought to be, and not as "Gud" and "Sams," as they often are.

Mannerisms are just as likely to be as irritating as mispronunciations, and again are more noticeable in others than in ourselves. I am sure that one of the best preachers of the generation which is passing away is not aware that he is for ever easing his collar by putting his finger between it and his neck. That is not a beautiful gesture, and has no meaning except that his collar is too small for him. A congregation need not be informed about a matter like that.

I might say so much about all this that you would never take up preaching, and I should never dare to preach again. So I shall say no more, except that God and the Gospel demand our best in every kind. As craftsman we should respect, as all true craftsmen do, our materials and our tools, and we should spare no effort to produce something that is as near our own ideal as hard work can make it: something into which, as all craftsmen do, we have put ourselves.

III

THE PREACHER AS TEACHER

III

THE PREACHER AS TEACHER

LORD REITH in his autobiography, *Into the Wind*, describes the impression his first glimpse of the front line made upon him in the War of 1914–18. He had some duty or other that sent him on ahead of his battalion, and he was eager to see what the front line was like. A corporal conducted him down a road which, he warned him, was sometimes swept by machine-gun fire, into a turnip field. A hay-stack was burning nearby: there was a moon. Soon a line of little lights appeared, stretching right and left in the darkness ahead. The front line, he was told. And this is what he says about it: "Spots of light from fires, hurricane lamps and candles: supremely moving in terms of what they signified. War cabinets, munition works, patriotic speeches, national efforts of every kind: all the gigantic machinery of the Empire at war; patrol ships, bases, depots, railheads, hospitals, clearing stations; G.H.Q., Army Corps, Division and Brigade headquarters: it all fined down in the end to a thread of twinkling lights."

So does all the ecclesiastical machinery of Assemblies, Conferences, Presbyteries, Theological Colleges, Church Offices, Committees, Congregations, Bible

Classes, Woman's Guilds fine down in the end to a thread of twinkling lights in offices, factories, workshops, schools, colleges, homes. If that front line is not adequately manned, how can all the machinery of the organised Church be justified? In this case the front line stretches not as the 1914-18 front line did, from the North Sea to Switzerland, but right across the world.

I have spoken of the preacher as evangelist, and have said that the object of our preaching is that God should be given the chance to make contact with our people. A further aim is that our people, evangelised, should themselves be evangelists.

This is where the preacher as teacher comes in. I need not emphasise the need—never more pressing than to-day—for the lay members of our congregations to realise their responsibilities for staying the advance of secularism and extending Christ's hold on the counsels and consciences of humanity. Nor need I point out that this is a task that our younger members, in particular, must face. But do they know much, if anything, of the story of the Church, or what the Creed has to say for itself? Can they give the answer to the man who says that "it doesn't matter what a man believes as long as he lives a decent life"? Do they know what is really at stake in the conflict of present-day ideologies? Attacks are constantly made both openly and insidiously on the whole Christian position. How many of our people are capable of defending that position with knowledge, let alone making any effective counter-attack?

The need for more teaching from the pulpit cannot be gainsaid. There has been far too little of it.

Quite obviously most of a preacher's teaching must be done elsewhere than at the ordinary services of public worship, and is best done in Bible classes, young people's fellowships, study groups and the like. In such more intimate circumstances we can be colloquial, invite questions, clear up difficulties, explain the technical terms of theology and the vocabulary of religious experience. We are apt to take it for granted that the terms we use in the pulpit and which constantly occur in our worship are understood. That this is not so any minister will soon discover who takes the trouble to investigate the situation, particularly as regards the younger generation. Nor need I remind you of the gulf that has been left too long unbridged between what we learn in theological colleges and what is often held concerning the Bible, by many devout Christians, and is still taught in Sunday schools and in meetings of young people.

Evangelism—far from ruling teaching out—is a poor thing unless there is teaching in it. Yet there is need for more systematic instruction than can be given in more or less disconnected inspirational sermons. If such systematic instruction is not given from the pulpit, many of our people will never be instructed at all. One difficulty about that is that many preachers, equipped, no doubt, with knowledge, have little skill in imparting it. Apparently they forget that they are dealing, not with a class, but with a congregation: not with people who are accustomed to listen to lectures, and have brought notebooks with them, so that, by burning the midnight oil, they may, at least, make an effort to understand what they have heard. They are not dealing with those who *have* to attend, and, unless they obtain a pass mark in examinations, will have to repeat the lectures.

Obviously preaching from a pulpit is different from teaching from a college desk. In a recent issue of a magazine I saw a picture of two girl undergraduates gazing after two dons—were they professors?—and one was saying to the other, their heads together, so as not to be overheard, "A couple of text-books wired for sound." An apt description of what the teacher in the pulpit should at least strive *not* to be. There are, of course, preachers as well as professors who are born teachers. I do not profess to be one of such. I can only tell you what my congregations have taught me, what they have appreciated and found helpful, what I have done in the way of systematic teaching and why I have done it.

Our people are constantly in touch with those who think that we are still holding the whole line of verbal inspiration from Genesis to Revelation: who are quite ignorant of what the Bible really is or sets out to be: who are quite sure that there is in the Bible a view of the Universe which is completely untenable by intelligent people to-day. It is nearly forty years now since a senior officer in my own regiment (I suppose for want of anything better to do) tackled me in the Mess about the intellectual honesty of educated men, like myself, who were entering the ministry of the Church. I asked him what he thought it was we believed, and whether he thought people like myself would spend the only life we had to live in practising a lie. No; he did not think so ill of us as that; but honestly now, could we really be surprised that people like himself had given up believing that the Bible was the Word of God? That gave me an opening to ask whether he would like me to tell him the views about the Bible commonly held by ministers to-day? He would. We talked for nearly four hours, he asking questions, and I giving him the best answers I could. At the end, when it was time for bed and the stars were at their brightest over the camp at Hamadan (the ancient Ecbatana), he said two things I still remember. One was, "Why have I not heard all this before?" and the other was "If what you say is true, then I am missing the greatest thing in the world." That was over thirty years ago, and still there are multitudes to-day who would ask the same question and make the same confession. Even amongst our devoutest people there are still those who are not too sure that criticism has not undermined the authority of the Bible, and who could give no reasoned answer to the cynic, to the sceptic or to the genuine seeker after the truth.

From my own experience, I know that there is appreciation for systematic teaching about the Bible—about the making of the Old Testament—about how the New Testament came to be written, emphasis being laid on this, that both are written in an ancient Eastern idiom, and that both are products of faith. How glad our people, as a rule, are to be shown that the Bible, when stripped of everything that is accidental and temporal, confronts us with eternal truths about man, life, the world and God. How glad they are to be assured that the question so often is, not "Can that have happened?" but "Is that a true thought"? Myth, legend, poetry have their place as well as history in the Word of God. Why not, then, have a series designed to show what the Bible is, and the best way to read and understand it? Picture it as a library representing the best of a people's writing for over a thousand years. No one would normally expect a library to be composed of works of equal interest and value, and no one would read right through the volumes just as they happened to be arranged on the shelves. One would expect an ancient library to contain legend and poetry and history and philosophy, and one would look first at the backs and the title pages to discover just what class of literature a volume belonged to before reading it. In the case of this library there are no such titles in gold on the backs, and no such information on the title-pages. It will therefore be your business Sunday by Sunday to supply these wants as far as you can. You will build up week by week a picture of men grappling with the mystery of God, seeking to understand His character, to interpret His will for and His dealings with themselves and their people, pouring out their own faith, doubts, and aspirations, collecting what they have discovered about the world He has made and the purposes for which He has made it— and doing all that and more in history, legend, poetry, prophecy for over a thousand years. If the inspiration of the Bible is not verbal (as who having any acquaintance with the original texts can think it is?); it is something better. The writers are men of whom it can be said that they are not only on their part seeking God—but on His part being sought by Him. They are in touch with a wisdom greater than human. They are expressing insights and intuitions and responding to impulses and inspirations that have their source outside and beyond their own minds and souls. The Word of God came to men in this living and continuous process, as how better could it have come, if they were to remain men at all, and if they were to be capable of speaking to us, who are separated from them by so many centuries? The living and continuous process, of which the Bible is the record, culminated in an experience of God as not merely inspiring, but indwelling fully in one who spake as never man spake. Christ never wrote a line; He trusted to men's memories of Him; He allowed them to form their own impressions, to reach their own conclusions and to write them down, just as God had allowed them to do from the beginning. The ways of God are singularly homogeneous. Shouldn't we expect them to be? Could we begin to understand them if they weren't? Begin, then, by taking down the Gospels: describe them, and show that they are the place where reading this library, called the Bible, should begin, so that we may have a standard by which to measure the other books of whatever kind, as to their authoritativeness concerning the character of God, the nature of man, the relationship there is between the two, and what God has in mind to do with us and for us and through us, if we will allow Him.

What is required is something "popular." Do not despise popularity. It is extremely difficult to be popular in the right sense of the word, and there is nothing to be ashamed of in making the attempt. Did not the common people hear him gladly? Don't you think He must have been "popular"? If we try to follow Him, at least we must do our best not to be dull. What we are saying must be so clear and real to ourselves that we can express ourselves in simple language, and in such a way as to convey our living interest in our subject to those who are listening to us. We have something that is infinitely well worth saying. We have not merely to tell a story: we have a story to tell.

Under the title, "The Bible for To-Day," I have given several series (seldom more than five or six addresses in any series), on successive Sundays, and have dealt in each with Old Testament stories. One series dealt with the Creation, the Fall, the Flood, the Tower of Babel, the destruction of Jericho. Another with the story of Moses, shirking none of the difficulties that crop up in modern minds, about the crossing of the Red Sea, the Ten Words, the Manna, the Pillar of Cloud and Fire. There was no talk about dispensations (a concept I can never understand) and no spiritualising of the ancient narratives (a practice which makes confusion worse confounded). At least an attempt was made to make the stories live and to tell them as if they recorded events that happened only yesterday.

Another series was called "How God got His character" and in it the development of the idea of God was traced until it culminated in the Christian revelation. May I say here with gratitude that I have very seldom been taken to task for using the word "myth" when dealing with the early stories of the Old Testament, and that I attribute that to the endeavour I made always to be positive and constructive in all I had to say. In my experience it is only criticism which leaves nothing of any value behind it that rouses opposition and resentment.

I do not think that we ministers realise how interesting to our people college lecture material can be

made. Why not give them New Testament introduction, determined that you are not going to be dull?
Make everything as personal as possible—say what *you*
think. I called such a series "Read the Bible with Me."
I dealt in the first address with the New Testament
as a whole, the order in which the books were written,
how natural it was for the Epistles to be written first,
what were the antecedents of the Gospels and why.
The second address was concerned with Paul and letter-
writing as the obvious means to his hand for keeping
in touch with, and instructing, the churches he had
founded; with some of the problems of faith and
conduct that worried the first Christians and the
Apostle as well. Then followed addresses, first on the
four Gospels separately, then in succession on Acts,
on Hebrews, and on Revelation, in which I told as
much as I could, in half an hour, of the authorship,
purpose and value of each. It was quite a lengthy series,
but it came to an end too soon. The material of these
addresses is all adaptable for Bible classes and for
lectures at summer schools and teachers' conferences,
but my point is that it is material which the average
Church member in the pew at a service of worship
finds interesting, provided it is presented to him in a
popular way.

Apart from such teaching as substitutes right for
wrong ideas of the composition, inspiration and
authority of the Bible, congregations value being
shown that the Bible is not just a collection of texts
for sermons. Nothing is more appreciated than to have,
say, one of the prophets dealt with, not chapter by
chapter, but under subject headings. Take Amos, for

example, and in three lectures you can give a very fair résumé of his teaching thus:

A Prophet speaks to us

1. *On the kind of world he lived in*: where men had forgotten their dependence on nature and each other. Draw out parallels in the world of to-day.

2. *On the wrath of God*. The book begins in a blaze of Divine anger. What makes Amos' God angry but inhumanity, cruelty and the devaluation of human beings? Have we been too ready to drop the fear of God out of our religous thinking? Do we know nothing of the wrath of God to-day?

3. *On the only religion that is worth while*. Amos is not very respectful to "religious" people—perhaps we need prophets like him to bring back power to the Church. For a religion that does not make better men and women and a juster and kinder world is not worth all the trouble and expense involved.

Or take a New Testament book like the Epistle of James. Call your series, "This Business of Living," and you will find James rich in suggestions about life in general, about temptation, about personal relationships, about faith and life, and how they hang together.

Or take the Book of Revelation. Rescue it from the hands of the cranks. Your people will be most interested in what you have to say about Apocalypse as a special type of literature; about the reason for its development, and about the meaning of the symbols it employs. With plenty of books of sound scholarship to help you, you can do something to earn the gratitude of your congregation by giving them at least some understanding of this difficult but rewarding tract for our times.

I would not weary you with suggestions, but I would emphasise how important it is to gather things together, so that your congregation is not fed on scraps. The chief need is that they should see Christ in something like His full proportions and significance. Have a series on "The Portraits of Christ" in the New Testament: Matthew's Mark's, Luke's, John's, Paul's; and after an interval follow it with a series on "The Self-portraits of Christ": "I am the Vine—the Bread of Life—the Good Shepherd—the Way—the Light of the World." A series on the "Personal Interviews of Christ," e.g. with Matthew, Nathaniel, Nicodemus, the Samaritan Woman, the Rich Young Ruler, will help to impress on their minds the understanding and the influence of our Lord as he deals with these varied types.

May I suggest a series on what our personal debt to Him is? I had a short series on these lines, which was appreciated, viz.

Our Personal Debt to Christ

1. For introducing us to ourselves and to each other. We need to see ourselves as Christ sees us, and to realise man's place as over nature but under God, as Christ and the Bible realise it, before we can begin to build the new world men and women have set out to build in these crucial times.

2. For not laying down the law. Christ gives us freedom of mind and conscience. The Christian life

is not a matter of rules, but of a spirit, and with that freedom come both dignity and responsibility.

3. For reconciling us to God. Without Christ we are working against a moral universe: with Christ we are working with it. People are often worried about the meaning of "atonement" until you express it in some such way.

If you deal with the questions asked by and addressed to Jesus, you will cover a great deal of ground. "Questions of the Great Question-master" are particularly rewarding, e.g. "What shall a man give in exchange for his soul?" "Why doth this generation seek after a sign?" "Who is my mother and my brethren?" "What would ye that I should do for you?" Do not make the series too long. Come back to it after an interval.

The chief questions, of course, for all of us are: What does it mean to be a Christian? What are the Christian standards? How should a Christian behave? What does following Christ mean for us to-day in our complicated society? We must give all the help we can to answer such questions, and is there any better way of doing so than by dealing with the Ten Commandments, the Sermon on the Mount, and the thirteenth Chapter of First Corinthians? Such series can be given more than once (if you remain in one church long enough) with advantage. They shed all the light we can possibly get on what it means to be a Christian, and they do not make it sound too easy a business either. They are not so much answers to our questions as challenges to our souls, and that is a great deal better for us really than definite answers. Our people will never know that

Christ offers a cross for them to carry till they realise the exacting nature of His demands. The only other suggestion I can give you is that if you deal, say, with the seven deadly sins in their original form, you may follow these up, before very long, with the same subject given a modern slant: the titles were given me years ago by a friend. (I may have slightly altered them.) Here they are:

The seven deadly sins of the Modern World.

> Pleasure without conscience.
> Cleverness without character.
> Science without humanity.
> Wealth without work.
> Industry without morality.
> Politics without principles.
> Religion without reality.

As well as for answering questions about Christian character and conduct, your congregation will be grateful to you when you shed light on words that are familiar. Quite recently I did a series on the Lord's Prayer and earned more vocal gratitude for it than for any other that I remember. The Prayer is the family prayer—"Our Father"—and after an address introducing the Prayer as such, comparing the versions in Matthew and Luke, and seeking to explain where "for Thine is the Kingdom and the Power and the Glory" comes from, I explained the structure of the prayer as falling under two main heads: (1) the rights of the Father and (2) the rights of the children. (I owed the idea to Canon A. W. Robinson's little book, *The Way to Pray*.) Then I gave addresses on successive Sundays on—

1. *The Rights of the Father*

(*a*) To respect—Hallowed be Thy name. And

(*b*) To obedience—Thy Kingdom come, Thy will be done in earth, as it is in heaven.

Two sermons on these subjects, and three on—

2. *The Rights of the Children*

(*a*) To food—Give us this day our daily bread.

(*b*) To forbearance—Forgive us our debts as we forgive our debtors. And

(*c*) To protection—Lead us not into temptation but deliver us from evil.

Within that framework, how much we can say that is helpful to those who use the Lord's Prayer often without realising more than a fraction of its wealth of meaning.

All the series I have so far suggested have been "doctrinal," but none of them have been devoted to any formal statements of the Church's faith. Whether we use it in our services or not, our congregations ought to be able to repeat the Apostles' Creed. How many congregations in the Church of Scotland can? I suggest then, a series on the Apostles' Creed. Show how all creeds are only, at best, the imperfect statements of truth that are beyond the reach of our thoughts and our words. Show the Apostles' Creed growing out of controversy in the endeavour to conserve the essential verities of the faith, and to keep the Church in line with the revelation which gave it birth. Express sympathy (if that is the way you feel about it) with those who would revise it and bring it, as they think, more up to date, but put the case as fairly as you can for leaving it as it is.

Sermons on the Creed can, of course, be very dull. I have found that I am extremely dull when I set out to be the competent theologian. (Am I an exception in this respect?) As I look back on such series of a theological kind as I have given at intervals, I find I have taken refuge in such titles as "Why I Believe in God the Father," "Why I Believe in God the Son," and so on, and the personal note has helped to keep the treatment from being heavy. Or I might announce a series—"A Preacher Takes Stock." In such a series I should give the reasons that count most with myself for believing in the Incarnation, the miracles, the Second Coming, prayer, immortality. Where I am aware of other people's difficulties I should confess, if such is the case, that I share them. But I should not confine myself to defending the faith. I should point out that sceptics believe what is quite beyond my capacity for believing, and I should end with the reminder that Christian belief is like casting a vote in an election. Having listened to what the other side has to say, you have to make up your own mind. As for myself, I cast my vote for the Church, which has been going now for a long time and has accumulated a great deal of experience; and that it is which weighs heavily with me. Theology thus becomes *my* theology, and, being a living thing to me, is more likely to be a living thing to those who listen to me. So far as I am aware, mine is a fairly orthodox theology. Certainly it is more orthodox now than when I was younger. I can only think that is because I know so much less!

One important fact we ought to recognise is that we may be quite out of touch with the difficulties which confront people to-day, both as regards the content of the faith and as regards carrying it into practice. So why not ask for questions to be sent in to you? A series dealing with those questions always arouses interest. You will get questions about the Bible, the Creed, prayer, the failure of the Church, missions, and Sunday games: in fact, most of the questions that might have been asked a generation ago. But you may get questions which are quite new, and, when they deal with Communism and Christianity I suggest that what we have to stress is that Communism is a challenge to Christian civilisation to set its house in order, and that since, by definition, it excludes God and religion, it takes all freedom, value and dignity from the human soul. One does not need, moreover, to debate Marxism or Leninism or any other "ism" to condemn the methods used to further world revolution. These are the first-fruits of leaving God and religion out of the count. Yet there is one point at least in the Communist campaign which it behoves us to notice—namely, that where a Communist is, there is the front line. If we are to see the survival of Christian ideals and values in the world of to-morrow, then there must be that thread of twinkling lights where Christ's forces are confronting the enemy— materialism, selfishness, irresponsibility—at every point, ready to defend, eager to advance. Our business as teachers, under God, is to pass on to our people such resources of faith, knowledge, and love as will make them good soldiers of the Lord Jesus Christ.

IV

THE PREACHER AS MINISTER

IV

THE PREACHER AS MINISTER

I AM concerned here, sermons apart, with some of the more important aspects of the preacher's work. I shall deal first with the preparation and conduct of services of all kinds.

Happily in recent years the importance of the element of worship in Church services has been increasingly recognised. This is evidenced by our churches themselves, which, whether they be new or old, are becoming more beautiful and more obviously houses of prayer. It is also evidenced by the wide use that is being made of the *Book of Common Order* drawn up by the Assembly's "Aids to Worship" Committee. The minister of the Church of Scotland may well feel that this book has taken a heavy weight of responsibility for the conducting of any kind of service off his shoulders, and we are all grateful to the Committee for the work they have done.

Whilst, however, such developments are certainly on the right lines, there is need, I think, for a note of warning. To place the pulpit to the side and to give the central position to the Communion table does not absolve us from continuing to give preaching the central place in our Scottish worship; to place an order book in our hands does not absolve us from continuing to put our own best into the preparation and direction of all the services we are called upon to conduct.

That is the point of view I shall present for your consideration in this lecture. I can only speak from experience of the less liturgical kind of service, but I think that what I have to say will apply to any service that is at all in line with the usual practice of the Church of Scotland.

With the Order of Service before us, we set out to make our preparation. We are to choose items of praise, select passages of Scripture, and prepare the prayers. I would suggest that since in our tradition the sermon is an integral part, and indeed as important a part as any in the whole service of worship (our Scriptural authority for that is that we are required to love God, not with heart and soul only, but with mind as well), the subject of the sermon should strike the note for the whole service, and that praise and prayer should time and again strike the same note. That does not mean that the hymns should be taken from any one section of the Hymn-book, but it does mean that in our selection of hymns, as of passages of Scripture, we have in mind the production of a particular effect. While preserving the variety which will make the service interesting and expressive of different worshippers' moods and needs, we are building up something that is a unity. The selection of praise is the preacher's business. By all means consult the organist as to the tunes. (There is no virtue in poor tunes, or in those that are unsuitable for congregational use.) The praise should be your selection, with the organist's help; not his selection, with or without yours. We are, of course, greatly dependent on our organists and choirs. They are our colleagues, and we ought to let them know how much we appreciate their help. If we happen to have a good organist and a good choir, we ought to be very grateful. But it may sometimes be necessary to persuade even a good organist and a good choir that choir-singing, however beautiful, is not a substitute for congregational praise.

Probably I have been spoiled by having in Wellington a church where there is a tradition of congregational praise. I certainly know by experience the difference it makes to preaching when there is no such tradition. Congregational singing prepares the way of the Lord as nothing else does. I am not belittling choir singing. On an August Sunday some years ago, I preached in one of our most famous cathedrals. There was a great crowd of people—mostly strangers, I imagine—who, as I sensed from the atmosphere, were initially more interested in looking round than in worshipping God. The service proceeded on its way, and as the time came for me to go to the pulpit to preach, I felt myself becoming increasingly worried and unhappy. I was just, so to say, another one of the performers, and it was my turn next. . . . Then the choir sang, unaccompanied, "God be in my head and in my understanding," and the atmosphere changed. What a change! That was really the moment when the service of worship began. So I do not belittle what a choir on its own can do for a service.

But such a sudden change of atmosphere should not be necessary in a congregation where visitors and sightseers do not predominate, and it is never necessary where the congregation sings. What besides encouraging organist and choir in the right direction can a minister do about it? I suggest he should stand throughout the singing, and he should not stand dumb unless he has not a note of music in him. He is part of the worshipping congregation, and the sight, if not the sound, of him singing will help others to overcome their diffidence about joining in. Why should the preacher sit down when the congregation rises up? The fact that the preacher is standing may remind him that the congregation is standing too; a salutary reminder, since in most pews there is not the same amount of room as there is in the pulpit, and standing therefore is more difficult, especially for those who are older than the preacher. Four or five verses of a psalm are enough, and most hymns can be cut if necessary, and with advantage, to a similar length.

As for the Scripture lessons—chosen carefully to bear on the subject of the sermon—they should not exceed from fifteen to twenty verses. If a passage is at all difficult, preface it with a short word of explanation. Even when this is not necessary, almost certainly some word or phrase will be obscure. Take time to make the meaning clear at any rate to yourself, so that your reading will have the best chance of conveying the meaning to others. But if the meaning is not clear to you, then find out what it is, and let the congregation into the secret. The Bible, after all, is meant to be understood. For most of our reading from the pulpit, the Authorised Version is certainly best, but where a modern translation has the advantage in clearness, and is dignified, why not use it? And do learn to read. Reading is, of course, quite a considerable art, and it will be a good day for you when a member of your congregation tells you that your reading moved and uplifted him. Do not try to make the Bible sound any different from any other kind of great literature. It will produce its own effect if it first produces that effect on you. Take pains to learn to read well.

The advantages of writing our prayers—whether we read them or not—are mainly these. We can make them short and concise. We can avoid clichés and repetition. Dated and put away, they can be used again and again, and in most cases we can improve them every time we use them. Keep all prayers short. People cannot and do not listen to long prayers, and in any case God does not hear us for our much speaking. We want people to pray along with us, and not merely listen to us. Therefore we must be short. Quite a short prayer may take an hour or even two to write, but the work involved is worth while. It is not unusual for people to thank one especially for the prayers, and that is an encouragement when they are silent about the sermon. The great prayers of the Church should be used, but great care should be taken with them, and with books of prayer designed to help us. The language of such prayers is sometimes archaic, and, if not un-natural to you, at least it is not natural to your fellow worshippers. The language of prayer should certainly be as dignified as we can make it, but we ought to remember that we are leading the prayers of the con-gregation, and incidentally also teaching them how to pray. I envy those who have the gift of prayer, but I think that working hard, using with judgment and discretion all the helps we can get from published prayers, and keeping the needs of the congregation constantly in mind, we have a fair substitute for that gift.

In particular, I am sure we do well to keep thinking of the congregation all the time we are preparing our prayers. Otherwise, they are apt to be merely the expression of our own needs and moods. Even if we only know the thoughts that are uppermost in the case of one or two, it is more than likely that, in giving expression to these, we shall also be expressing the thoughts that are uppermost in the minds of others who are unknown to us. What we seek to do in prayer is to lift our people into the presence of God. To do that we must first identify ourselves with the hopes, fears, joys, sorrows, strength, and weakness of the busy, burdened, complacent, doubting, kindly, lonely folk who are in the pews. And then we must find language which has the quality of wings—language simple and sincere (our prayers are to be real prayers, addressed to a real God, about the real issues of life), but with something of poetry in it; language shot through with that real emotion which we call compassion—compassion for all sorts and conditions of men.

Each of us must use his own gifts and discover his own method of prayer-preparation, deciding for himself which words and phrases are too archaic or too exotic, and which Biblical allusions are too recondite or too hackneyed to suit his purpose. But let us remember this: that, even if our people would never dream of interjecting an "Amen" at intervals, or even of saying aloud "Amen" at the prayer's end, unless they feel what "Amen" means in their minds and hearts, our prayers will have failed to do what prayer in the congregation should do, and the service of

68

worship will be so much the poorer because of that.

In a simple order of service, is there room for a children's address? I think there is. I cannot speak to very young children with any satisfaction, either to them or to myself, and except at special children's services I do not try to do so. But I regularly speak to boys and girls of from eight to twelve years of age, and when I do I have a shrewd suspicion that even the youngest take in quite a lot that would seem to be above their heads. What are the pros and cons? First the cons:

1. There are so few children that it is not worth while.
2. They have their own service in the Sunday School.
3. Such an address is an interruption and a distraction in the service of worship.

And the pros:

1. Children like to come to church if there is an address and a hymn for them.
2. Parents appreciate a service where their children are provided for in this way.
3. Children have been known to bring their lapsed parents back to church because they themselves were eager to come.
4. Children's addresses are remembered when other addresses are forgotten.
5. Practice in giving simple addresses is practice in writing sermons for adults. These are often too difficult and too dull.

69

6. Such addresses are useful for passing on moral lessons, Bible instruction, education in worship, of which our adult members are none the worse.

I have no doubt in my own mind that the pros have it. Remember I am not saying that an address of the kind would be suitable in every Church and in every congregation, but where the service is non-liturgical and there are children present, I do not think an address to them need be an interruption or spoil the atmosphere of worship. Of course, if one is to secure the attention of children, it may be necessary to speak in a way that will raise a smile on the faces of grown-ups. I see no objection to that. When did God object to a smile? We should glorify Him more if we smiled oftener and made our Church services more interesting and attractive as a result. Of course, if any man sets out to be funny in a children's address, he will only succeed in being cheap.

Perhaps the chief objection to the children's address is really this: it is very difficult to come by a good children's address, and to do it every week. I have often wished I had never begun the practice, but if I were to give it up I wonder how many parents and others would come and ask me to begin again? I commend children's addresses to all the ministers who feel they cannot do them, for I am sure it is they who need to do them most. Our preaching on the whole is too abstract and too difficult. There is a story, possibly apocryphal, of a well-known professor whose own preaching, always distinguished, grew in simplicity and effectiveness as he grew older. He must have been a fairly young man when he was present at a service conducted by a young minister who had a popular following and a crowded church. After the service someone asked him if he had liked the children's address. He said in reply: "Which of them?" In spite of that jibe, I am convinced that the best sermons for grown-ups have at least some of the qualities of children's addresses, and that there is no need to apologise for them, except on the ground that we do them badly.

More people are likely to be in church on Communion Sunday than on any other day, except perhaps Remembrance Sunday. I need not point out that this gives the preacher a special opportunity. His preaching should be on the most central themes of the Christian faith, and he should be in no doubt about the impression on mind and conscience which the dignity and solemnity of our traditional Scottish form of Communion is able to produce even on the minds and consciences of the most careless of worshippers. Nothing has been better done in our *Book of Common Order* than the form of the Communion Service, yet I suggest that not only is the form too long, but there is room for making our own changes in it, or for adapting it with the help of other forms which are available, in order to bring its meaning more closely home to our congregation. I may be wrong, but I think I have found that the kind of preface that appeals to my congregation as well as to myself, runs something like this:

After such introductory sentences as "I am the Bread of Life: he that cometh to me shall never hunger, and he that believeth on me shall never thirst," "Behold I stand at the door and knock," the congregation is invited to partake of the symbols of Christ's sacrifice, in such a manner as this:

"Ye that do truly repent of your sins, are in love and charity with your neighbours, and desire with your whole heart to follow the commandments of God, draw near with reverence, with faith and with thanksgiving, and take the Supper of the Lord to your comfort.

"Come, not because you are strong, but because you are weak. Not because any goodness of yours gives you a right to come but because you need mercy and help.

"Come because you love the Lord a little and would like to love Him more.

"Come because He loves you and gave Himself for you.

"And now that the Supper of the Lord is spread before you, lift up your hearts and minds above all your cares and fears, and let this bread and wine be to you the token and the pledge of the Grace of the Lord Jesus Christ, the love of God and the fellowship of the Holy Spirit, all meant for you if you will receive them in humble faith."

With such a simple introduction there is, I think, no loss of dignity, and there is a gain in the more personal approach. I realise, of course, that there are differences as between congregations, both in the places of their worship and in the traditions which they have inherited, but it does seem to me that there is a definite advantage in thinking for ourselves as to what best will produce the effect Communion is intended to produce. We should not be slaves to any book or to any set forms.

That applies also, of course, to marriage and baptismal services. Again the *Book of Common Order* is most helpful, and keeps us on the right lines generally. The Baptismal Service is one of the most moving that we are privileged to conduct. It should therefore be the most simple and the most human. If we accept that view, then it seems to me that it becomes difficult to say, as the *Book of Common Order* enjoins us: "The Sacrament thus instituted is a sign and seal of our engrafting into Christ; of forgiveness of sins by His blood, and regeneration by His Spirit; and of adoption, and resurrection into everlasting life." All that is doubtless true, but it is questionable if the parents of a child are much impressed by so many big words and big ideas.

The service is a service of thanksgiving, of dedication, and of consecration. It is expressive of the fact that the child is entrusted to the parents to bring up in the Christian faith and life, and that God Himself and the Church are ready to help them. We need not employ anything but the simplest words to say so, and I do not think that we should use the same words every time we baptise children. I therefore suggest that you make your own order and adapt it according to circumstances, leaving your book behind when you conduct the service. If you remember that you are Christ's representative, that He took little children in His arms, laid His hands upon them and blessed them, if you see something of the wonderful thing that a child is, and remember that you and all your congregation were once as clean and as promising, you will not fail to make the Baptismal Service as moving as it ought to be.

As for the Marriage Service, again I suggest that we should not be tied to the *Book of Common Order*, or indeed to any book of order that we may possess. The words of Scripture in our own book are appropiate and beautiful, although I scarcely think that we need to read a passage such as this: "For the husband is the head of the wife, even as Christ is the head of the Church: and He is the saviour of the body. Therefore as the Church is subject unto Christ, so let the wives be to their own husbands in everything." Are such words likely to make any kind of impact on a bride and bridegroom, or on the guests who are assembled in the pews at a wedding service? Why not get together a selection of short passages from the Old and New Testaments? I first heard this particular selection at a marriage at which I was assisting many years ago now, and I have used it often since:

"Put off thy shoes from off thy feet: for the place whereupon thou standest is holy ground."

"A man shall be as an hiding place from the wind and a covert from the tempest, as rivers of water in a dry place: as the shadow of a great rock in a weary land."

"A virtuous woman is a crown to her husband: her price is far above rubies: the heart of her husband doth safely trust in her. She will do him good and not evil all the days of her life."

"A woman that feareth the Lord she shall be praised."

"Bear ye one another's burden and so fulfil the law of Christ. . . ."

Then follow with 1 Cor. xiii, "Love suffereth long and is kind," and end with the lovely passage from John xv: "As the Father hath loved me, so have I loved you. . . . This is my commandment: that ye love one another as I have loved you."

It seems to me that if we always remember that in these sacraments God is drawing near to people who are more in the mood then than at any other time to realise their need of His grace, we shall not fail utterly in what is and what ought to be one of the high occasions of their lives.

The same approach should be made to Funeral Services and for the same reason. What an opportunity to do what is our main business—namely, to give God His chance to make living contact with His children at a most impressionable time. The passages of Scripture appropriate to the Funeral Service are amongst the most beautiful and the most moving in all literature, and the message of the Gospel, which assures us we are not wandering dust and the grave is not our goal, that we are God's children and precious in His sight, that we are going whither we cannot see, but we never leave our Father's house, that we are the children of eternal love and underneath us are the everlasting arms, bring inexpressible comfort to the bereaved.

It is therefore more than a pity if we ever fail to allow the Gospel to do its beneficent work. We are in the presence of the final mystery of all, and we are the vehicles of God's own comfort of light and life and peace to men; therefore let us be attuned when we conduct Funeral Services to both the human and the divine. I am sure that if we remember that the departed is never just a man or a woman who has come to the end of the road, but one who has struggled and hoped and dreamed and suffered, and loved and been loved, a sinner indeed, but now in the merciful hands of God, we shall not fail to bring the comfort of the Gospel home to all who are present. A beautiful thing was said by a lady about a Funeral Service for a dear dead sister:

"It took all the hurt away." That should be our aim.

We may have public funerals to conduct for those who have done good service to Church and community. Ever since, years ago, I saw one of our daily papers, wishing to pay tribute to the deceased, reduced to quoting what the officiating clergyman had said in his prayer, I have always paid a tribute after the singing of the opening psalm or hymn, so that a reporter could use, if he chose, what I said, and so that, later, copies of what I said might be sent to the family by means of the congregational magazine. It seems to me that funeral services for ministers are often lacking in this very respect. The tribute need never be fulsome. It only needs to be real to be right.

As I look back on what I have been saying, it seems to me that the lesson I have been taught—whether I have always profited by it or not—is this: that the more thought I have given and the more of myself I have put into all that I was called upon to do, the more it has been appreciated. No trouble taken beforehand is ever wasted, and no want of trouble or seeming want of trouble is ever unnoticed.

That observation does not merely apply to what we might regard as important occasions. It does no kind of honour to any meeting or to the minister himself if he is asked to open with prayer and he sets off on a rambling and interminable jumble of unctuous words.

The Pastoral side of the minister's work is of paramount importance. The closer and more frequent his contact with his people outside the pulpit, the greater will be his influence while he is in it. The trouble is that in city churches especially, congregations are so scattered that it is a physical impossibility to keep

76

touch, as ideally a minister should. A minister who has sermons to write, Bible classes to prepare for, organisations of various kind to keep an eye on, marriages and funerals to conduct, letters to answer, extra congregational meetings, Presbytery meetings and committees to attend has his hands more than full. The result is that a good many of us who are ministers of large congregations have uneasy consciences about neglected visitation, and an uneasy conscience is one of the worst of companions.

This is not the place to do more than suggest a remedy, but I may express my own opinion that the only effective remedy is a radical revision of the whole set-up of the Church in cities. There might well be many fewer churches, so that the remainder might be more adequately staffed, and I think it would be a far better thing for the Church to go thoroughly into this question in the interests of efficiency now, rather than to have to do it in order to meet the exigencies of the economic situation and the decline in numbers of candidates for the ministry. At the present moment, too many men are struggling, doing many things less well than they ought to be done. Preaching as well as pastoral work suffers from the over-multiplication of tasks laid upon the individual minister, who is often lonely and loses heart. We shall have to wait till that is changed, but changed, I think, it must be. Meanwhile, we must carry on as best we can. Whether your Church be in city or in village, and whether it be large or small, give visitation a principal place amongst your duties, and do it as conscientiously as you can.

It is often a dreary enough exercise to climb tall stairs and find locked doors, and it is often a question one asks when one gets home again, whether visiting is really worth while. But then there are the visits one pays where one has done something to lend courage, where a simple act of prayer has brought tears of gratitude, where the welcome one received has done good to one's own soul. It is not then as an irksome duty, but as a source of satisfaction and happiness that I counsel you to be conscientious and constant in visitation. The more contacts we have with our people the better—the better for them, I should hope, but certainly the better for us. They have more to teach us about the problems of faith and life, about courage and loyalty and all else connected with the human spirit, than we can learn from books. It is not unlikely that, as we get to know our congregation, we shall discover that there are those in it for whom religion is a shallow enough profession, but we shall also certainly find that there are those in it who are more able to strengthen our faith than we are to strengthen theirs.

V

THE PREACHER AS MAN

V

THE PREACHER AS MAN

THIS is not an easy subject to deal with, and I am perhaps less fit to deal with it than with any that have gone before it. We are not concerned with the evangelist or teacher or minister as such, but with the man who is all three: with the kind of man he is in his contact with others, and the kind of man he is in himself. Difficult as it is to treat such a subject, there can be no avoiding it.

The kind of men we ministers are is perhaps of greater importance to-day than it ever was. Time was when we Scots were a nation of church-goers; the place of the Church in the community was unchallenged, and the minister was respected because of his office. That time has almost gone. Sunday is not what it was. Church-going is no longer a fixed habit even with church members. It may be too much to say that for the majority of our Scottish people the Church means little or nothing, for old institutions and old habits die slowly; but at least it is true that very many turn upon the church uninterested or critical eyes. The minister nowadays has to justify himself and his profession in a new kind of way. What place he holds in the esteem of the congregation over which he is set, and of the community of which he is a member, he must win for himself, and the Church gains or loses according to the measure of that esteem.

It is therefore right that we should realise that what people think of us is important. Not so important, indeed as what God thinks of us, but if men think little of us there is no guarantee that God will not agree with them. I do not want to suggest that we should go out of our way to win popular approval. There is good Scriptural warrant for not wanting all men to speak well of us, and on the highest authority we know that it is a blessed thing to be persecuted for righteousness' sake. I do suggest, however, that it may not be always for righteousness' sake that we find ourselves so often a misunderstood and misrepresented class, offering the caricaturist, for one, a good deal of material to work on. We need not take the caricaturist too seriously. His art demands exaggeration as part of its technique. But the pompous and unctuous type of parson who appears on the stage and screen, the effeminate and spineless type, not to mention the grim and censorious type, are not yet by all accounts extinct. Such never have done much to enhance the dignity or usefulness of our profession. They certainly will not do anything of the kind to-day. The sincere, hard-working, self-effacing, natural and human minister (and I am glad to say that, so far as I know, most ministers are such) is more than ever the strength as well as the best advertisement of the Church.

Perhaps I should explain what I mean by "human". Apparently it still comes as a surprise even to Church-people to discover that ministers have most of the weaknesses they deplore in themselves, and some of the virtues they respect in each other; that they are sympathetic rather than censorious; that they find pleasure where other decent people find it; that they make no claim to any particular degree either of faith or virtue, but are, in both respects, strugglers like other people, and know it.

When members of a congregation have discovered that their own particular minister is, in that sense, human, they are prepared to give him a hearing which they will deny to other men. His may not be preaching that is intellectually distinguished (all the better, of course, if it is), but it will be preaching of a kind that interprets the compassion and attractiveness of Christ, and is therefore worth all the other kinds put together.

Here is a man, the older folk feel, who is neither conceited nor aloof. He is young and he is not omniscient; he is old but he is not dried up. Here is a man, the younger members feel, who does not speak as if we were "miserable" sinners (they not knowing the original meaning of "miserable"—as why should they be expected to?), but just as ordinary sinners like himself: if *he* finds religion a real and a helpful thing, as he says, there must be something in it. Others, whether old or young, are glad to listen to one who does not seem to consider it a kind of blasphemy to ask questions; who admits that he does not know all the answers; who is neither glib nor dogmatic. He lives a sheltered life (that is what they all think), but he sympathises with us who are not so fortunate. He says the world is wrong, as of course, it is, but he has no easy remedy to suggest, and he appreciates our difficulties in putting Christian principles into practice.

When that is the kind of impression made, there is

not merely a minister, but a man in the pulpit. If in his preaching, such a man exalts Christ as Lord and Saviour, he is bound to exercise an influence both wide and deep. He is in fact, on the way to being loved. All the best ministers have been loved, and not all have been "good" preachers, in the accepted sense of the word.

To be human is not only, I submit, the first requisite for such preaching as wins home to men's businesses and bosoms, but it is the indispensable requisite for dealing with people when they are in trouble. They will confide more fully and openly in the minister who is a warmly human fellow creature than in the minister of whom all they know is that he is a representative of the Church. And he, for his part, will not be so unthinking as to speak the merely professional word, the correct and pious platitude. He will be ready, of course, to pray with the sufferer or the penitent sinner, but a hearing ear, a pressure of the hand, an offer of practical help—if that is called for—are worth all that he can say. In any prayer or counsel he may offer he will confess his own need for help, and he will give this witness: that he himself has found that help in God. Jesus wept at the grave of His friend, and though He did more than we can ever do, yet at least that is within our power.

When the trouble is moral—as it sometimes is— we may well remember also what Christ did when confronted with a sinning woman and an outraged crowd. He bowed His head and wrote in the dust. It was not the woman who worried Him most. He said to the crowd: "Let him that is without sin among you cast the first stone." He said to the woman: "Neither do I condemn thee: go in peace." What a warmly human Saviour and Lord! He must ever be our example. We shall not be following His example if we class as the worst sins those that are most obvious. It seems to have been overlooked that Christ was harder on the Pharisees than on the publicans and sinners. Spiritual sins—pride, jealousy, enmity, bitterness and all want of charity—are not unknown in our churches, and we should be a great deal harder on them than on what are commonly and quite wrongly regarded as the greater sins of the flesh. Naturally, when dealing with the sins of the spirit, the human minister will never dream of claiming or implying that he himself is exempt from these. The only claim he can make is that, confronted with Christ, his own sins of the spirit are rebuked, and that only by being continually confronted with Him can he, or anyone else, hope to overcome them.

It is not only important for the congregation that we should be human; it is also important for the Church and for what those outside and lost to the church think of it. I find, among newspaper and magazine cuttings I have kept, the outpourings of soul of an American Bishop. "There are times," he says, "when one is a little ashamed of being a clergyman. . . . I am not ashamed of the ministry itself. I am ashamed to be identified with that which the other men in the smoking compartment conceive it to be. In the back of their heads is the conviction that most ministers are engaged in snooping into other people's business, regulating other people's morals and endeavouring to standardise other people's brains. They regard all ministers alike as professional members of 'the society of moral uplifters.' They conceive of the ministerial life as narrow, if not bigoted, as joyless and severe, censorious, rigid, ungenerous in its judgments, petty in its aims.'' A formidable list of prejudices to be sure, and fairly accurate: not, indeed, as a description of the facts about ministers and the ministry, but as a description of the conception of the facts in many minds. Sometimes at least I have felt like the Bishop, and have wished it were possible for the people who have such prejudiced views to meet a selection of the ministers I know well, or that they could spend, say, a week in a manse or in a church hut or canteen.

An Earl Haig car-park attendant in Glasgow, disabled in the 1914–18 War, whom I see about once a week has asked me on several occasions if I know a certain minister. (I only know his name.) And he has told me more than once that he had had a very unfavourable opinion of ministers till he went during the last war, in some capacity or other, to help in a canteen. The minister was in charge of the work, and the attendant had lived beside him for some months, had seen him at all hours, in all kind of circumstancess, and had liked him—his humour, his willingness to do chores, his decency, his friendliness. The result was that, as he said, he had changed his opinion of ministers. Week by week I now bask in the genial goodwill towards my profession in the heart of a simple man. I confess it is quite a pleasant experience. Do not misunderstand me. I do not mean that being indistinguishable from other decent men is enough qualification for a minister to be a man, or for a man to be a minister: to be natural, to be friendly, to have a sense of humour, to be unshockable is much, but men also expect ministers to be consistent and to practise what they preach. They respect them also when on occasion they are outspoken. Am I right in thinking that it was Dr. John Kelman who, in an Edinburgh club, heard a man boasting that, as for him, he did not believe there was a God. And Dr. Kelman said something to this effect: that no man would boast of that unless he had a reason for hoping that there wasn't. Men respect consistency, courage and outspokenness. That is perhaps what some ministers forget who want to prove that they are good mixers and, without meaning to, let themselves and all the rest of us down. A padre in a battalion mess told the kind of story that is generally regarded as unsuitable for a drawing-room. The Colonel said—as only Colonels can (or perhaps they share the gift with sergeant-majors?) "I know what *my* job is, but I am d——d if I know what *yours* is." We have our job. Men know more or less what that job is, and they respect us when we respect it and when they see us trying to do it.

One of the truest tests of whether a minister is remembering too much that he is a minister and too little that he is a man is what the young people think of him. When I asked a friend how his new minister was getting on, he said: "Oh, all right, but in So-and-So's time, the children used to run across the street to meet the minister. Now they run across the street to avoid him." I knew the minister a little: quite a good fellow. I asked what was wrong. The answer was: "He never forgets he's a minister." His collar did more than denote his profession: it came between him and the exercise of it. It was throttling him.

The American practice of wearing the collar only on official occasions has much to commend it. It is not only necessary that we be natural with people, but that they should be natural with us. And when they see this tell-tale collar, people are usually on their guard. Travelling years ago between Calcutta and Bombay with my valise (name, rank and regiment, printed in block letters) on a rack above my head, I had an experience which illustrates this. The man directly opposite was a Scot and, as it turned out, one of the talkative kind, who, in spite of notions to the contrary, do exist and in quite considerable numbers. Another man, immersed in a book, was the only other occupant of the compartment. The Scotsman had apparently been in India for a good many years, and addressed himself to me in order to enlighten me on the subject of the country and the people. Most of his remarks were derogatory, or, alternatively, to say the least, ill-informed. The man was, as I knew, not representative of the best of our countrymen in business and the Services, and I was sorry he should give himself away as he was doing before two strangers. I felt I had to say something to indicate to him how radically I disagreed with him, and so I thought I should tell him, to begin with, that I was a theological student, and that I took an entirely different view of India from the one that he had been airing. In fact, that I took the view—to put it shortly—of the missionary. The man in the far corner looked at me over his book and said "I am with you, sir. I am an American Y.M.C.A. secretary." Distances are great between stops in India, and, whatever there are now, there were no corridor coaches in those days. So our friend, now in the minority, had to listen to what we had to say for some time. A clerical collar on either the American or myself would have deprived that Scot of much enlightenment.

Perhaps I have said enough about being human: there is, of course, no standard pattern. Some of us are more reserved than others. Some are more self-conscious. Some suffer fools gladly and some have not that gift. We all have to do what we can with the gifts which we have. But there is no reason why we should not make efforts to overcome any weaknesses of which we are aware, and to cultivate, in especial, tolerance, not only for all possibilities of truth, but for all types of humanity. That, plus the faculty of listening without appearing to be either superior or bored, will go a long way to establishing right relationships with our fellow men.

We might sum up what I have been trying to say on the basis of my own experience about what it means for the minister to be a man. It means to be human, to be natural, to be sincere, to be consistent and to be Christian.

There is an idea abroad that it is somehow easier for ministers to be Christian than it is for the rest of men. I am not so sure that there is any foundation for such an idea. We have the same temptations as all flesh is heir to, and some perhaps that are peculiar to our calling. It is not easy to avoid insincerity when we have to preach whether we are in the mood or not. We tend to become professional, and there is such a thing as professional jealousy. We can become so engrossed with petty affairs and petty people that some pettiness gets into ourselves. We are apt to become self-assertive when out of the pulpit, because, when we are in it, no one dares to contradict us. The besetting sins of ministers have been said to be whining, shining and reclining. If there is any justification for such a list, it must be said that the items in it are not of equal importance. "Whining" or the sing-song voice, though unfortunate and a hindrance to effective preaching, is not so serious as either of the other two. Who was it said that "you cannot preach Christ and be clever at one and the same time"? "Shining" is being clever. Cleverness attracts attention to the preacher, and that is bad not only for the Gospel, but for him. The spot-light should be on Christ, and the minister who draws attention to himself is forgetting the reason for his existence. The fact that we ministers are so much masters of our own time, as few men are, is the explanation for "reclining" in this unholy trinity. It simply means laziness. To realise that we are privileged to be on our own should make us more conscientious than ever in the use we make of our working hours. My own experience leads me to think that the danger is not so much that most of us are not busy enough, but rather that we are too busy. We have not enough time to read, to think, to pray. And yet we can all deceive ourselves about that. Are we as busy as we think? Should we not decide on the relative importance of our multifarious occupations, and establish and observe some order of priority? Perhaps I have said enough to explode the idea that it is easier for a minister to be a Christian than it is for other people.

What, then, of the devotional life of the preacher? If the great pianist could say that a day's want of practice made a difference, noticeable to himself, and that a week's want of practice was noticed in the gallery, that is likely, within limits, to be true of us if we neglect our private devotions. Here again, however, no rules can be laid down. We must find out for ourselves what we can do. Some counsel getting up early in the morning. You cannot do that and stay up late at night. And if that is your habit, and you are busy all day in sermon-preparation, letter-writing, visiting, attending meetings, you will not have much time left for private study and prayer. When there is—as is so often the case these days—the added burden of a large house and no help, things get even more difficult to arrange so that a quiet time can be found. Yet it must be found at all costs.

May I make a suggestion about this which may be helpful? I do not find it possible, or natural, to spend many consecutive minutes exclusively in what is called "private meditation," but I do find that I can give my own soul the benefit of many of the things I have to do as I go about my day's work. If I read the Bible with a view to preparing a sermon, am I not at liberty to read it for my own profit at the same time? Indeed, if I do not do that first, how am I going to prepare anything that will help my congregation on Sunday? We need not do what I have seen a Roman Catholic priest do in a bus—and admired him for it. There he was, apparently oblivious to the starting and stopping, the coming and going, squeezed up against the side of the bus, reading his Office and saying his prayers. Nor need we do what I have seen a keen evangelical layman do in the train, with a well-thumbed Bible open on his lap. But we can take thoughts of God with us wherever we go. We can remember Whose we are and

Whom we serve at all times and in all places, and whether we are walking along the corridors of hospitals, or climbing stairs, or ringing door-bells, we can ask a blessing on ourselves and on the visit we are about to pay. If we make a habit of recollecting Christ at every point of need, and in every kind of service we seek to do, I think we shall be supplementing quite effectively the spiritual nourishment we take in on our knees and with the Bible or a book of devotion in our hands. All will be needed to enable us to fulfil the injunction: Be Christian.

There are, of course, other helps, other means of grace. There is the help that praying members of our congregation give us. We are prayed for by some every day. There are brother ministers, stronger, wiser and more Christian than ourselves, to whom we can go for counsel and help. We are singularly unfortunate if we have no close friends to whom we can confess our hopes and fears, our failures and shortcomings. Greatest of all such means of grace, I shall only illustrate by an incident quoted by my predecessor in Wellington. Dr. G. H. Morrison tells us that there was a time in Principal Rainy's life when he was the most hated man in Scotland. Scarcely a week passed in which the newspapers had not a venomous attack upon him, and all the time, neither in face nor in temper, did Rainy show one trace of irritation. One day Dr. Whyte met him and asked how he managed it. His reply was: "I am very happy at home."

May I end what I have been saying about the preacher as man, with this: that no man, whether minister or any other, can be as good a Christian as he should be, or do as effective work for Christ and his Church as he might, if he rates his gifts and his deserts too highly. He must be prepared to meet with discouragement and failure and to occupy a very small place in the purposes of God, and he must have within him that resilience of spirit that keeps him going under the most difficult conditions. I think that is the meaning of Christian humility, which is a basic characteristic of the Christian. Humility of this kind has this practical advantage: that, combined with charity, it covers a multitude of sins. As an aspect of the humility which thus combines with charity, we should develop, or keep if we have it already, the ability to laugh at ourselves. May I tell you a ridiculous story that is true? I was taking my first Session Meeting in my church in London. The Session was composed of as impressive a company as I had ever presided over, all of them a good deal older than myself. They did not know me, and I did not know them. I knew that, naturally, they were observing me closely. I wished, of course, to make a good impression on my first contact with them. I was very nervous and felt ill at ease. I said to myself: "It is sheer nonsense being nervous like this. I must take myself and the situation in hand." And so I ventured on a joke. It was not a good joke. No one laughed except myself, and that was due not to amusement, but to nervousness. I laughed and leant back in my chair. The joke had fallen flat and so did I, for the chair disintegrated under me! A complete collapse. What a beginning! What lack of dignity! How vexing at my first Session Meeting! The amazing thing was that before I could pick myself up I was laughing in real earnest, laughing at myself, laughing at the whole situation, and moreover, as a result, laughing with the whole company. We were friends and brothers from that moment. I do not take any credit to myself out of this story, but I do take this out of it: that if we can, at least occasionally, laugh at ourselves, God lets us down gently. I have put the lesson to good use. I have had to, for I have made many mistakes.

I have been saying that the fact that you are to be ministers marks you out from other men. Please, I have urged, not in the wrong way so that other men will think you are different from them, and, please, not so indistinguishably that it is only your collar which differentiates you from them. Before you are a minister you must be a man and a Christian. You must show that you are both, not only in the street and in the railway compartment, but in the pulpit, where you must speak in a natural, unstilted, unaffected way about things that really matter, with a humility that becomes your youth, because you cannot possibly know everything yet, and that still becomes you when you are old, because by then you will have proved to yourself that you do not know anything at all. Even after you are ordained and you are celebrating Communion, you will do that best when it is quite clear to all that here is a man who is a sinner and who knows it, a man offering to sinners like himself the love and the grace of God.

And now you are within measurable distance of setting out on a task the most significant and the most satisfying of any offered to man: the task of ministering to men, women and children who are surrounded by a great mystery, who are all restless until they rest in God, who are all in the grip of powers too great for them until they know the power of God, who are all heading for the undiscovered country whence no traveller returns. To them you are to hold forth the word of life, to offer the light of faith, to tell the story of redeeming love, to welcome to the communion and fellowship of the Holy Spirit. No profession has so wide, so deep and so moving a range of interests and occupations. Neither you nor I are fit for so exalted a work, yet God has called us to it and we must give to it and to Him the best we have to give.

Now unto Him who is able to keep us from falling and to present us faultless before His presence with exceeding joy; to the only wise God our Saviour, be honour and glory, dominion and power, both now and for ever. Amen.

Date Due